Earthquakes and Volcanoes

A Survival Guide

John Townsend

www.raintreepublishers.co.uk

Visit our website to find out more information about **Raintree** books.

To order:
☎ Phone 44 (0) 1865 888112
📄 Send a fax to 44 (0) 1865 314091
💻 Visit the Raintree bookshop at **www.raintreepublishers.co.uk** to browse our catalogue and order online.

First published in Great Britain by Raintree, Halley Court, Jordan Hill, Oxford OX2 8EJ, part of Harcourt Education.
Raintree is a registered trademark of Harcourt Education Ltd.

Editorial: Lucy Thunder and Harriet Milles
Design: Victoria Bevan and Bigtop
Illustrations: Darren Lingard
Picture Research: Melissa Allison and Virginia Stroud-Lewis
Production: Camilla Crask

Originated by Dot Gradations Ltd.
Printed and bound in Italy by Printer Trento srl

The paper used to print this book comes from sustainable resources.

ISBN 1 844 43160 6
10 09 08 07 06
10 9 8 7 6 5 4 3 2 1

British Library Cataloguing in Publication Data
Townsend, John
Earthquakes and Volcanoes – A Survival Guide: Earth's physical processes
551.2'1
A full catalogue record for this book is available from the British Library.

Acknowledgements
The publishers would like to thank the following for permission to reproduce photographs:
Alamy Images/AM Corporation pp. 22–23; Alamy Images pp. 26–27 (Adrian Arbib); Corbis p. 13; Corbis/Reuters p. 15 (bottom); Corbis/Reuters 11 (bottom) (Yuriko Nakao); The Kobal Collection/Universal pp. 4–5; Science Photo Library p. 11 (top); Science Photo Library pp. 16–17 (Jeremy Bishop), 15 (top) (Gary Hincks), 6–7 (Ken M. Johns), 21 (right) (Peter Menzel), 29 (David Parker), 24–25 (Dr Morley Read), 18–19 (David Weintraub), 21 (left) (Ed Young).

Cover photograph of Los Angeles cityscape, reproduced with permission of Getty Images/Taxi.

The publishers would like to thank Nancy Harris and Harold Pratt for their assistance in the preparation of this book.

Every effort has been made to contact copyright holders of any material reproduced in this book. Any omissions will be rectified in subsequent printings if notice is given to the publishers.

Contents

Some words are printed in bold, **like this**. You can find out what they mean on page 30. You can also look in the box at the bottom of the page where they first appear.

What on Earth is happening?

"It was only a murmur at first. The sound seemed far away. What was going on? Soon, it sounded like a train passing through the house. The floor started to move and rumble. Everything began to shake. The room swayed.

"The TV fizzed and went out with a pop. By now the noise was a thundering roar. Books fell off the shelves. Then the shelves themselves fell down. There were thuds all through the house. This was scary! This was an earthquake!"

This person was describing how it feels to be caught in an earthquake. Would you know what to do in an earthquake? One day you may need to know.

▼ The scene in this photo is from a film about an earthquake.

5

The power of earthquakes

When a big earthquake strikes, the ground shakes. It shakes so much that buildings fall down. Cracks appear in the roads. Bridges can break.

But earthquakes are not always dangerous. Sometimes the Earth only moves a little. This is called a **tremor**.

Volcanoes often **erupt** where earthquakes happen. Volcanoes are cone-shaped mountains or hills. A volcano can throw up liquid rock, or **lava**, from deep inside the Earth.

To be safe from earthquakes and volcanoes you need answers to some questions:

- Why do earthquakes and volcanoes happen?
- Where are the most dangerous places?
- What are the warning signs?
- What should you do if a volcano erupts near you?

Read on to find the answers!

erupt	to break through a surface and burst out
lava	melted rock that comes out of a volcano
tremor	small earthquake

▼ This huge crack in the Earth's surface was caused by an earthquake in California, USA.

Did you know?

- In 1556, an earthquake killed over 800,000 people in China.

- In 1815, a volcano killed 90,000 people in Indonesia.

Inside the Earth

What makes earthquakes happen and volcanoes **erupt**? To understand, we have to look at the way the Earth is made.

The Earth is a bit like an egg. It has:

- a **crust** (a thin outer shell)

- a **mantle** (a thick layer of hot rock below the crust. In some places, the rock melts. The liquid rock is called **magma**.)

- a **core** (the centre of the Earth).

The Earth's crust is cracked into large pieces. If an egg shell is cracked, the insides ooze out through the cracks. In the same way, liquid magma can ooze out through the Earth's crust. This happens in places where the crust is very cracked or thin. These are the places where volcanoes form.

This picture shows the▶ inside of the Earth.

core	central part of the Earth
crust	outer part of the Earth
magma	hot liquid rock in the Earth's mantle and crust
mantle	thick layer of rock between the Earth's crust and the core

The large pieces of the Earth's crust can move around. These movements are what cause earthquakes. Earthquakes and volcanoes tend to happen near the cracks in the Earth's crust.

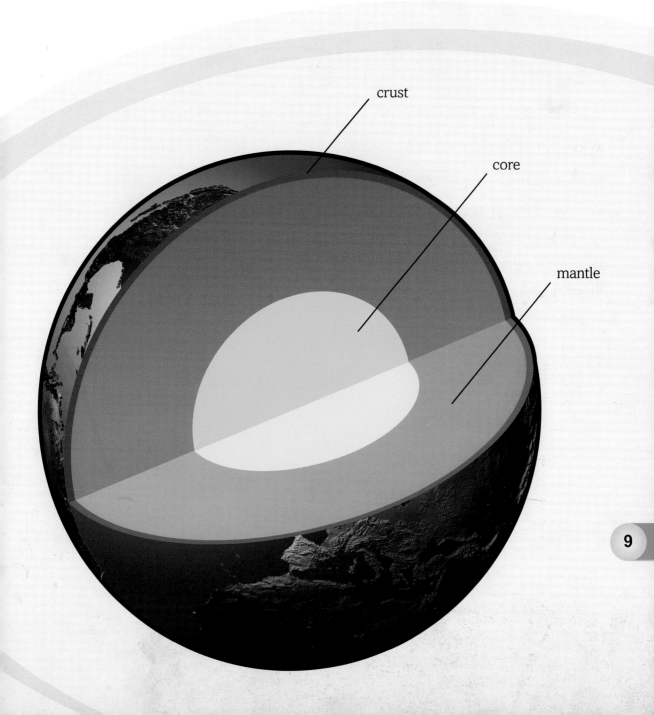

crust

core

mantle

The restless Earth

The huge pieces that make up the Earth's **crust** are called **plates**. These plates rest or "float" on top of the **mantle**.

The mantle is like thick, liquid plastic. It moves very slowly. The slowly moving mantle makes the plates move too.

Plates may:

- move apart from each other

- push into each other

- slide slowly past each other.

The edges of the plates are jagged. The edges may stick together for a long time. Then creak … crunch … BANG! They suddenly scrape past each other. This is when an earthquake happens.

If an earthquake happens under the sea, it can cause huge waves, called **tsunamis**. Tsunamis can travel for hundreds of miles over the ocean.

plate huge moving piece of the Earth's crust
tsunami great sea wave made by an earthquake under the sea

The Earth's plates

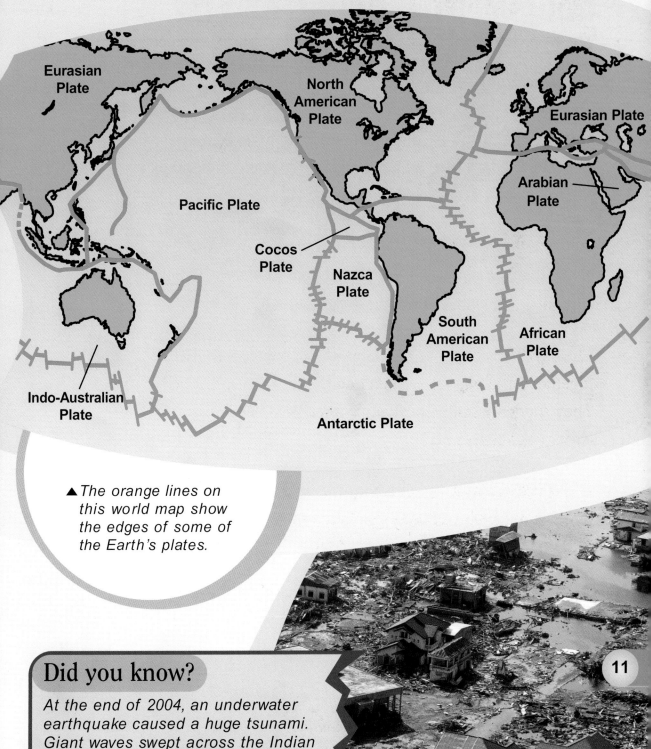

Eurasian Plate

North American Plate

Eurasian Plate

Arabian Plate

Pacific Plate

Cocos Plate

Nazca Plate

South American Plate

African Plate

Indo-Australian Plate

Antarctic Plate

▲The orange lines on this world map show the edges of some of the Earth's plates.

Did you know?

At the end of 2004, an underwater earthquake caused a huge tsunami. Giant waves swept across the Indian Ocean. Over 200,000 people died.

Danger zone: Ring of Fire

The biggest of the Earth's **plates** is the Pacific Ocean plate. It is as big as the Pacific Ocean.

Most of the Earth's earthquakes and volcanoes happen around the edges of the Pacific plate. Earthquakes happen where two plates are moving past each other.

Volcanoes burst through cracks in the Earth's **crust**. There are so many volcanoes around the edges of the Pacific plate that it is called the Ring of Fire.

Ring of Fire

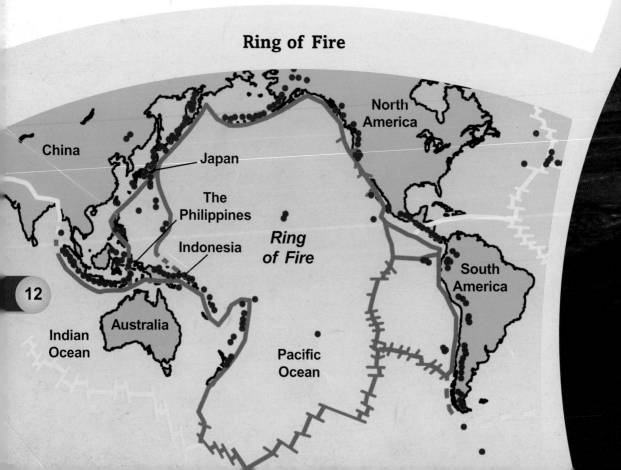

China

North America

Japan

The Philippines

Indonesia

Ring of Fire

South America

Australia

Indian Ocean

Pacific Ocean

12

The red dots on the map on page 12 show where volcanoes are along the Ring of Fire. It is not easy for people living in these places to avoid earthquakes and volcanoes.

▼ *Smoke often pours out of volcanoes along the Ring of Fire.*

Warning signs

Scientists cannot always tell when earthquakes will strike. But sometimes they can warn that an earthquake will happen soon. Scientists use an instrument called a **seismograph** to measure earthquakes.

In 1975, scientists in China were sure an earthquake was going to happen. No one could feel the **tremors**. A seismograph sensed them. Scientists gave a warning. The next day, an earthquake hit Haicheng in China. Because of the warning, people left the city. Many lives were saved.

But a year later, another earthquake struck without warning near Haicheng. It killed about 250,000 people.

Did you know?

San Francisco in the United States was almost destroyed by an earthquake in 1906. In 1989, another earthquake struck the same area. Scientists think that another big earthquake will hit the city in the next 30 years.

seismograph instrument used to measure and record movements of the Earth

Case

Pen

Roll of paper

▼ A seismograph is fixed to the ground. In an earthquake, the case and the roll of paper move around. The pen stays still. It draws the pattern of the earthquake on the roll of paper.

Volcano alert!

Scientists can often tell when a volcano is about to **erupt**. A volcano is fixed in one place so it is easier to study. Photographs taken from space can show volcanoes changing shape. This happens before they erupt.

Scientists who study volcanoes are called **volcanologists**. They climb on to volcanoes. They measure changes in the ground.

A volcano throws out liquid rock called **lava**. Lava is boiling hot! Volcanologists need to wear heat suits to be safe.

A heat suit will not protect scientists against lava bombs. These are huge lumps of melted rock that shoot into the air. Hot ash and deadly gases can suddenly shoot out, too.

volcanologist   scientist who studies volcanoes

▼ *Studying an active volcano can be a very dangerous job!*

17

Without warning

Sometimes volcanoes **erupt** without warning. On Sunday, 18 May 1980, Mount St Helens erupted. This volcano is in Washington State in the United States.

Ten minutes earlier, an earthquake had shaken the volcano. It made the north face of the mountain fall away. This caused the biggest **landslide** ever known. Tons of earth and ice crashed down into Spirit Lake nearby.

Gases had built up inside the volcano. Then the north slope of the volcano fell away. The **pressure** inside the volcano was released. It was like a cork popping out of a bottle.

Survivor's story

On 18 May 1980, Jim Scymanky and three other men were cutting wood in a forest near Mount St Helens. Jim described how "a horrible, crunching, grinding sound" came through the trees. Suddenly the air was full of hot, black ash. They were all badly burned. Jim was the only survivor.

landslide   when a mass of rocks or earth slips down a steep slope
pressure   force pushing against a surface

▼ When Mount St Helens erupted, 57 people were killed.

Measuring the power

Many earthquakes and volcanoes rumble all the time. They are not all dangerous.

Earthquakes come in different strengths. They can be small **tremors**, or great mega-quakes. Scientists measure how strong an earthquake is on a scale. It is called the **Richter Scale**. It gives an earthquake a score between 1 and 9.

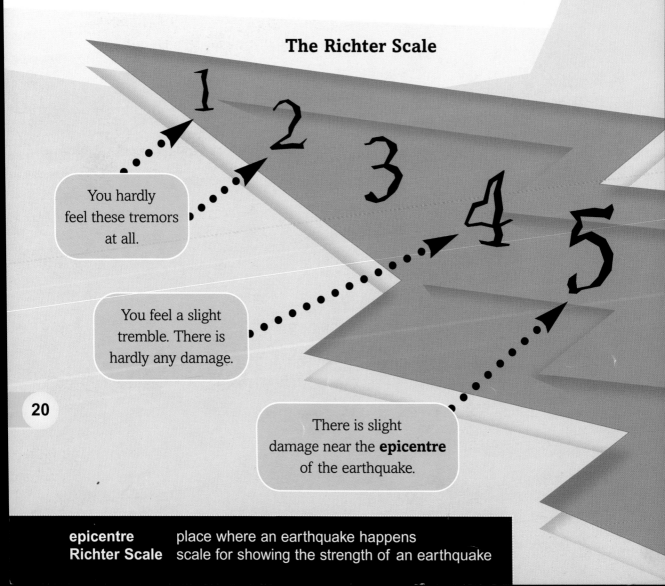

The Richter Scale

You hardly feel these tremors at all.

You feel a slight tremble. There is hardly any damage.

There is slight damage near the **epicentre** of the earthquake.

epicentre   place where an earthquake happens
Richter Scale   scale for showing the strength of an earthquake

**California
1994**

**Mexico City
1985**

There is serious damage 100 kilometres (62 miles) from the epicentre.

There is huge damage. Many people are killed over hundreds of kilometres.

Mega-quakes like this do not happen often. There is massive damage over thousands of kilometres.

6

7

8

9

There is damage to buildings within 10 kilometres (6.2 miles) of the epicentre.

21

Safe building

If you live in an earthquake zone, you need a well-built house. No building can be completely safe from earthquakes. But all buildings can be made safer. They need to be built with extra-strong materials.

In earthquake zones, many buildings are built on special pads. These pads can move with the shaking Earth. This stops the buildings from falling down. Some homes in Japan and the United States are built this way.

A special bridge

The Akashi-Kaikyo bridge in Japan was specially built to cope with earthquakes. The bridge should stay standing in earthquakes that measure up to 8.5 on the **Richter Scale**!

After-effects

The earthquake is over. The shaking has stopped. Is everything safe now? No, it is not!

Everywhere there are broken electricity wires and broken gas pipes. These can cause injury, death, or serious fires. There are broken water pipes, too. Dirty water soon spreads disease. This is a very dangerous time.

Did you know that volcanoes can even change the weather? In 1815, the volcano Tambora **erupted** in Indonesia. The next year was known as the "year without a summer". Tambora threw out thick clouds of ash. The sunlight could not get through these clouds.

The biggest bang

One of the biggest volcanic eruptions was Krakatoa in Indonesia. In 1883, it blew apart a whole island. It caused a **tsunami** that killed 36,000 people. A thick cloud of ash rose 80 kilometres (50 miles) into the sky. It affected the world's weather for several years.

▼ This is Quito, the capital of Ecuador. In 2002, the volcano Reventador erupted nearby. It filled the air with ash. People needed face masks to help them to breathe.

Survival

Learning about earthquakes and volcanic eruptions can help to keep you safe. It is important to know what to do if they happen. But you do not always have to worry about them.

Remember that most earthquakes are so small you cannot feel them. Many others do nothing more than rattle the windows.

Did you know that volcanoes can sometimes be good for you?

Some people live close to volcanoes. They do this because ash from volcanoes makes good, rich soil. The rich soil is good for growing crops. Also, streams on volcanoes can be hot. They give free hot water!

▼ *People can live very well near volcanoes. The soil around a volcano is rich and good for farming.*

Be prepared

In an earthquake, you are in danger of getting hurt by falling buildings. Follow this good advice to keep as safe as possible:

DROP down to the floor.

Take **COVER** under a strong piece of furniture.

HOLD on to the furniture. Be ready to move with it until the ground stops shaking, and it is safe to come out.

REMEMBER

- If you are in a HIGH BUILDING, and you are not near a table, go to an inside wall. Protect your head with your arms.

- If you are OUTDOORS, move away from trees, buildings, or wires.

- If you are NEAR BUILDINGS, duck into a doorway. Protect yourself from falling bricks.

- Be prepared for further earthquakes called AFTERSHOCKS. Take cover when they happen.

(Based on advice from the American Red Cross)

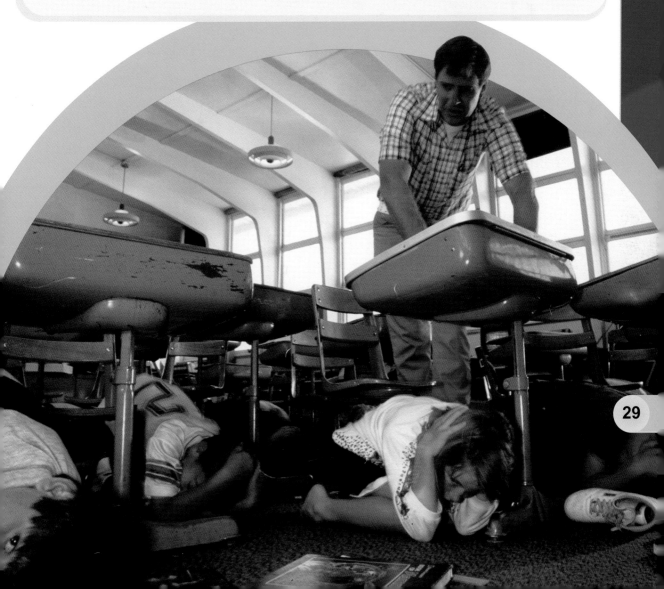

Glossary

core central part of the Earth. It is made mostly of the two metals, iron and nickel.

crust outer part of the Earth. The crust is made of solid rock. It is between 10 and 50 kilometres (6.2 and 31 miles) thick.

epicentre place where an earthquake happens. The epicentre is the point on the Earth's surface that is directly above where an earthquake starts.

erupt to break through a surface and burst out. Volcanoes erupt every year around the world.

landslide when a mass of rocks or earth slides down a steep slope. Landslides can be caused by earthquakes. They can also be caused by very heavy rain.

lava melted rock that comes out of a volcano. When lava cools it hardens into solid rock.

magma hot liquid rock in the Earth's mantle. Magma rises up through the Earth's crust and comes through the mouth of a volcano as lava.

mantle thick layer of rock between the Earth's crust and the core. In some places, the mantle is so hot that it is melted. This is where volcanoes happen.

plate huge moving piece of the Earth's crust. Earthquakes and volcanoes often happen where plates meet.

pressure force pushing against a surface. Pressure builds up under the Earth's crust. This causes earthquakes and volcanoes.

Richter Scale scale for showing the strength of an earthquake. It measures the strength with scores from 1 to 9. 9 is the strongest.

seismograph instrument used to measure and record movements of the Earth. This can tell scientists how powerful an earthquake is.

tremor small earthquake. Tremors often happen before or after a big earthquake.

tsunami great sea wave made by an earthquake under the sea. Tsunamis are rare, but they can cause terrible damage when they strike a coast.

volcanologist scientist who studies volcanoes.

Want to know more?

Books to read

- *Horrible Geography: Earth Shattering Earthquakes*, by Anita Ganeri (Scholastic Hippo, 2004)
- *Horrible Geography: Violent Volcanoes*, by Anita Ganeri (Scholastic Hippo, 2004)
- *DK Guide to Savage Earth*, by Trevor Day (Dorling Kindersley, 2001)

Websites

Try these websites to find out more about volcanoes and earthquakes:

- http://www.enchantedlearning.com/subjects/volcano/
- http://www.nationalgeographic.com/ngkids/0312/
- http://earthquake.usgs.gov/4kids/
- http://www.exploratorium.edu/faultline/

Find out more about the restless Earth, and how it can affect our weather in *Disappearing Mountain and Other Earth Mysteries*.

Rocks can be a lot more exciting than you might think! Find out why in: *Tales of a Prehistoric Sponge*.

Index